Sagebrush Steppe Vegetation Monitoring in Lake Roosevelt National Recreation Area

2011 Annual Report

Natural Resource Data Series NPS/UCBN/NRDS—2012/231

Jeffrey J. Yeo, Ph.D.
518 N. 350 E.
Shoshone, ID 83352

Thomas J. Rodhouse
National Park Service, Upper Columbia Basin Network
20310 Empire Ave., Ste. A100
Bend, OR 97701-5998

January 2012

U.S. Department of the Interior
National Park Service
Natural Resource Stewardship and Science
Fort Collins, Colorado

The National Park Service, Natural Resource Stewardship and Science office in Fort Collins, Colorado publishes a range of reports that address natural resource topics of interest and applicability to a broad audience in the National Park Service and others in natural resource management, including scientists, conservation and environmental constituencies, and the public.

The Natural Resource Data Series is intended for the timely release of basic data sets and data summaries. Care has been taken to assure accuracy of raw data values, but a thorough analysis and interpretation of the data has not been completed. Consequently, the initial analyses of data in this report are provisional and subject to change.

All manuscripts in the series receive the appropriate level of peer review to ensure that the information is scientifically credible, technically accurate, appropriately written for the intended audience, and designed and published in a professional manner. This report received informal peer review by subject-matter experts who were not directly involved in the collection, analysis, or reporting of the data. Data in this report were collected and analyzed using methods based on established, peer-reviewed protocols and were analyzed and interpreted within the guidelines of the protocols.

Views, statements, findings, conclusions, recommendations, and data in this report do not necessarily reflect views and policies of the National Park Service, U.S. Department of the Interior. Mention of trade names or commercial products does not constitute endorsement or recommendation for use by the U.S. Government.

This report is available from (http://science.nature.nps.gov/im/units/ucbn/) and the Natural Resource Publications Management website (http://www.nature.nps.gov/publications/nrpm/).

Please cite this publication as:

NPS 606/112476, January 2012

Contents

Figures

Tables

Executive Summary

Lake Roosevelt National Recreation Area (LARO) is one of 5 parks within the Upper Columbia Basin Inventory and Monitoring Network (UCBN) area that contains sagebrush steppe ecosystems. Five monitoring sites within Lake Roosevelt National Recreation Area, each containing 50 or 55 plots, were sampled in early June 2011 following methodologies described in Yeo et al. (2009). Three of the 5 sites are grazed by cattle annually in spring and in fall, and 1 site contains the Spring Canyon campground and boat launch. Cover of exposed soil, sagebrush, other shrubs, perennial native grasses, perennial persistent forbs, other native forbs, non-native invasive forbs, and non-native invasive grasses were estimated in randomly-located 1-m² plots. The weather in spring and early summer 2011 were unusually wet and mild. Cheatgrass (*Bromus tectorum*), a non-native, invasive annual grass, was ubiquitous across all 5 sites, and was the most frequently encountered plant at all 5 sites. Other non-native annual grasses, Japanese brome (*Bromus japonicus*) and bulbous bluegrass (*Poa bulbosa*), also were occasionally abundant. Dalmatian toadflax (*Linaria dalmatica*), an invasive noxious forb, was common at 1 site and present at other sites as were knapweeds (*Centaurea* spp.; also noxious, invasive forbs). Plots depicting sagebrush steppe in good condition were sparsely scattered within the 5 monitoring units indicating (1) the very limited extent of vegetation in good condition, and (2) the small patch sizes of good condition habitat. There were isolated patches of vegetation in several of the monitoring sites in which native bunchgrasses such as bluebunch wheatgrass (*Pseudoroegneria spicata*) and Idaho fescue (*Festuca idahoensis*) were dominant. Three of the 5 monitoring sites were sampled in 2009 and selected variables were compared between the 2 sampling years. Differences in cover estimates between the 2 sample years were few, and the wet, mild spring and early summer weather of 2011 likely contributed to higher cover of annuals with resultant lower estimates of exposed soil cover compared to vegetative conditions experienced in the drier and warmer weather of 2009.

Acknowledgments

We thank Ken Hyde, Chief of Resources and Interpretation at LARO, for making the arrangements for staying at Spring Canyon campground, and for taking the time to share his knowledge of the issues affecting sagebrush steppe in the park. Ken also reviewed an earlier draft of this report. Meghan Lonneker, UCBN GIS analyst, produced the excellent maps for the report.

Introduction

Sagebrush steppe ecosystems in the Upper Columbia Basin, prior to EuroAmerican settlement, extended across the eastern half of Washington and Oregon, and across the northern Great Basin of southern Idaho. Currently much of that ecosystem has been lost to development or substantially degraded as a result of livestock grazing, fire, non-native invasive plants, and recreational use. UCBN has identified the ecological condition of sagebrush steppe vegetation as a high priority vital sign and monitoring of its condition is central to its monitoring program (Garrett et al. 2007). A long-term monitoring program that provides for regular evaluation of the status of the health of UCBN steppe communities, and for identification of trends of ecosystem condition over time within and among parks within the network was implemented in 2008 (Yeo et al. 2009). The foundation of the sagebrush steppe monitoring protocol is a view of ecosystem health sustained by natural succession or natural variability within communities of native plants. Divergence of sagebrush steppe communities from these natural states (e.g., invasion of non-native plants, increased fire frequencies, long-term trends of increasing cover of exposed soil, declines in cover of principal native plants) signifies a loss of health, and provides the feedback to park managers for effective adaptive management strategies. Simple monitoring objectives follow directly from this view:

- Determine the status (current condition) and trends (change in condition over time) in the composition and abundance (cover) of principal native plant species in UCBN sagebrush steppe communities.

- Determine the status and trends in composition and abundance (cover) of principal invasive plant species, including annual grasses, in UCBN sagebrush steppe communities.

- Determine the status and trend in the amount of exposed soil (cover), a fundamental indicator of soil stability.

This report summarizes the data collected in 2011, and provides simple comparisons for selected parameters to the data collected in 2009.

Study Area and Methods

Figure 1. LARO monitoring area showing the 5 permanent monitoring sites (shaded yellow areas) with Roosevelt Lake to the north (Grand Coulee Dam just off the picture to the upper left).

LARO comprises a narrow band of terrestrial habitats surrounding Lake Roosevelt, a reservoir created by Grand Coulee Dam on the Columbia River. Sagebrush steppe communities occur principally along the southwestern periphery of the reservoir continuing upstream from the dam for about a dozen miles. Based on existing vegetation maps and ground surveys in May 2009, we identified 5 permanent areas ("monitoring sites") containing the largest contiguous patches of sagebrush steppe (Figure 1). Monitoring sites ranged from 8 – 41 ha (Table 1). Three of the monitoring sites (Neal Canyon, Ponderosa, and Spring Canyon East) are grazed by cattle during the spring and fall; the other 2 sites receive some recreational use with the highest use in the Spring Canyon West site that includes the Spring Canyon campground and boat launch. We sampled three of the monitoring sites (Crescent Bay, Spring Canyon West, and Spring Canyon East) in May 2009. All 5 sites were sampled during June 1-5, 2011. The intended sampling frequency for these sites is biennial.

Table 1. Monitoring site areas and sample sizes for Lake Roosevelt National Recreation Area sagebrush steppe monitoring, 2011.

Monitoring Site	Area (ha)	Sample Size (plots)
Crescent Bay	41	55
Neal Canyon	27	55
Ponderosa	9	50
Spring Canyon East	8	50
Spring Canyon West	19	50

Sampling procedures followed Yeo et al. (2009). Within each site, 1-m² square plots were located using the generalized random tessellation stratified (GRTS) spatially-balanced sampling design (Stevens and Olsen 2004). The GRTS approach provides for randomly located plots and good spatial dispersion across each site. Fifty to fifty-five plots were sampled within each site with more plots allocated to the larger sites (Table 1). Within each 1-m² plot, we estimated cover of exposed soil, and principal native plants and non-native invasive plants. Cover estimates were categorized into the following cover classes: 0, 1-5%, 5-25%, 25-50%, 50-75%, 75-95%, and 95-100% (Daubenmire 1959). Plant cover was defined as the natural spread of current year's growth outlined using a minimum convex polygon with small gaps included in the cover estimate. Exposed soil was defined as soil surface not overlain by plant cover, litter, and rock. Plant common names and their scientific names are listed in Appendix 1.

Plots that we considered in "good" condition were defined as having cover dominated by perennial native plants with no cover of noxious weeds, low cover ($\leq 5\%$) of invasive annual grasses – cheatgrass, Japanese brome, or bulbous bluegrass – and exposed soil cover $\leq 25\%$. These "good" condition plots are highlighted on the maps of each monitoring site.

For comparisons among monitoring sites, we used the Kruskal-Wallis analysis of variance on ranks test. Where data were available for comparisons between years for the same areas we tested for differences among selected parameters using the Mann-Whitney rank sum test. These two statistical procedures are useful non-parametric alternatives to the familiar two-sample *t*-test and one-way analysis of variance, suitable for the ordinal cover class data collected by our protocol (Higgins 2004). All comparisons were considered statistically significant at $P \leq 0.10$.

Weather

Long-term weather records for Coulee Dam show an arid period typically extending from May to October (Western Climate Data Center, 2011; Figure 2). In 2009, the arid period began about a month earlier than typical, and monthly precipitation was less and temperatures slightly warmer than average during the summer. Spring 2011 was cool and wet with some snow falling on the hills surrounding the reservoir into May (Ken Hyde, NPS, pers. comm.). Substantially greater precipitation fell during April and May 2011 than typical, and much greater than in 2009. Although the cool, wet spring and early summer likely delayed plant growth, it almost certainly contributed to increased cover of annuals and early season perennials. Note that weather data are derived from monthly summaries except for April through June 2011. These data were calculated from the raw monthly weather station records because monthly weather summaries were not available at the time of this writing.

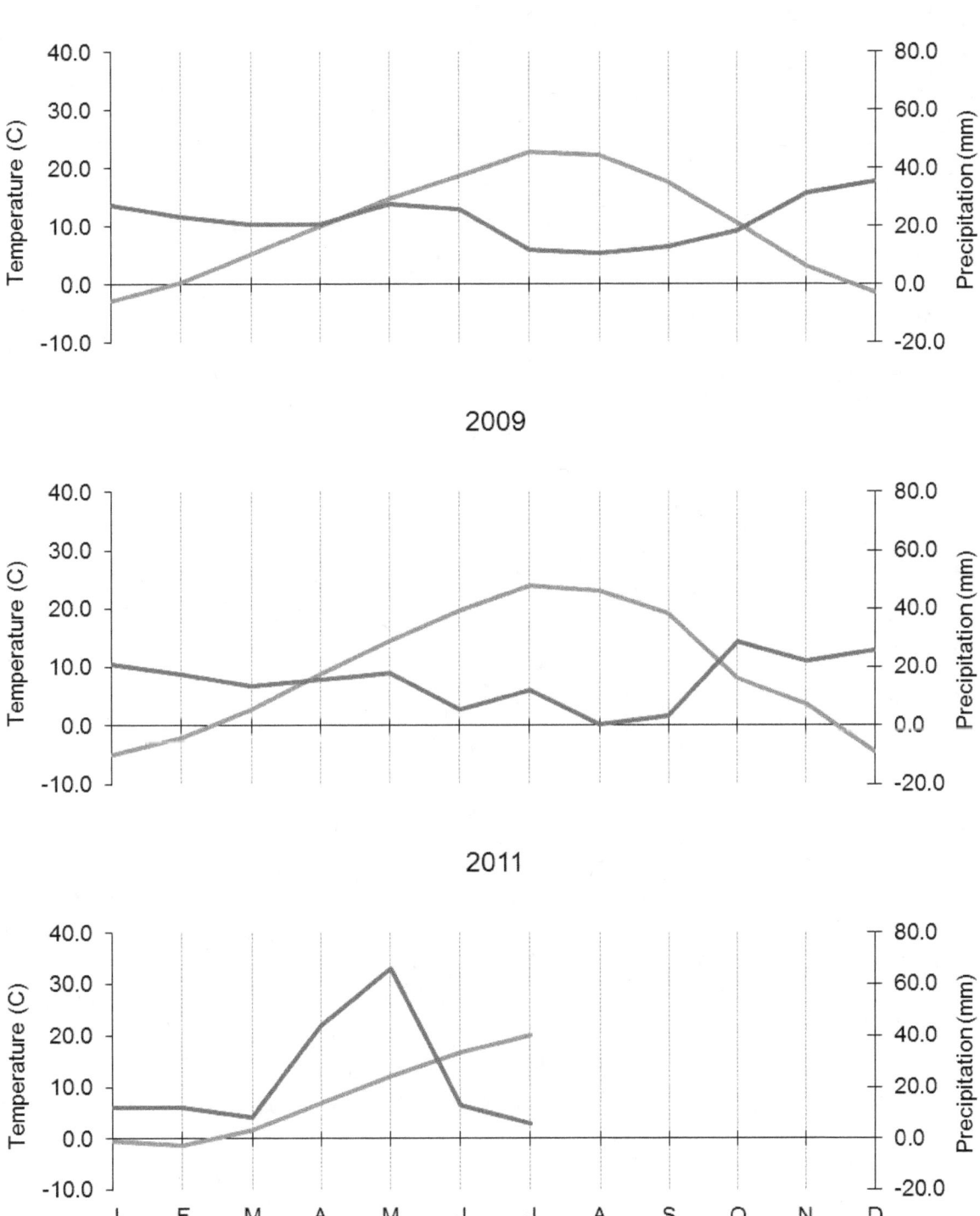

Figure 2. Climate diagrams (following methods described by Walter et al. 1975) for the Coulee Dam weather station within Lake Roosevelt National Recreation Area comparing the long-term (60 yrs) average monthly temperatures (red line) and monthly average precipitation (blue line) to temperatures and precipitation in 2009 and 2011. The period when the temperature line exceeds the precipitation line defines the arid period for plant growth.

Results and Discussion

Crescent Bay

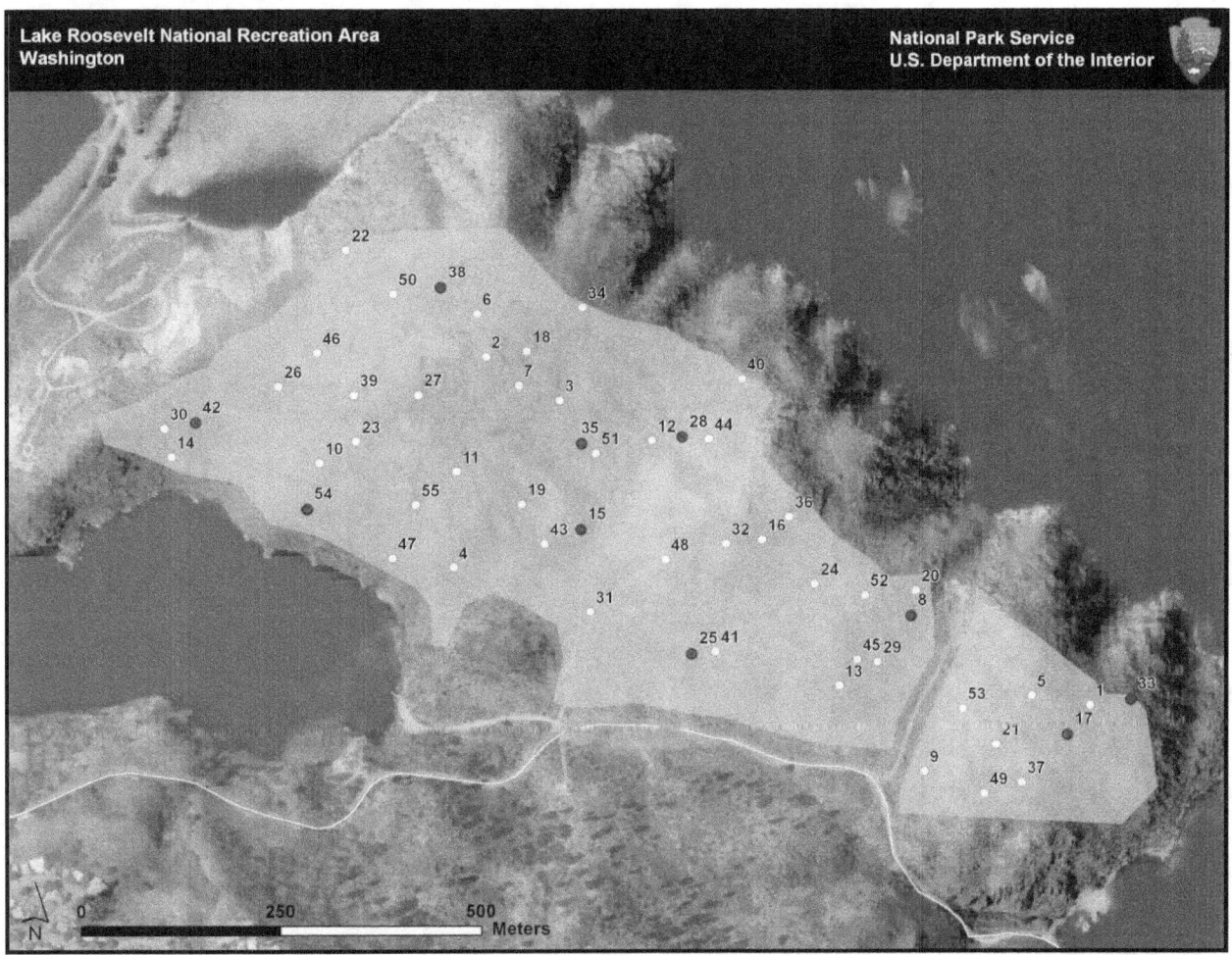

Figure 3. Crescent Bay monitoring site showing 2011 plot locations and plot numbers. Good condition plots are depicted by larger blue dots.

We sampled 55 plots in the Crescent Bay monitoring site on June 4, 2011 (Figure 3). Cheatgrass was the most commonly encountered plant (found in every plot – 100% frequency); cover values of > 25% occurred in 35% of the plots (Table 2). Japanese brome and bulbous bluegrass were encountered in a few plots mostly with cover < 5%. Big sagebrush (*Artemisia tridentata*) was the dominant shrub in the site, along with scattered pockets of rigid sagebrush (*A. rigida*) and threetip sagebrush (*A. tripartita*). This monitoring site appeared to have the most abundance of rigid sagebrush and purple sage (*Salvia dorrii*) of any of the 5 sites, although both species were only encountered in one sampling plot. Needlegrass (*Stipa* spp.) and Sandberg's bluegrass (*Poa secunda*) were the most commonly encountered native bunchgrasses. There were some areas within the site where bluebunch wheatgrass was abundant. Desert parsley (*Lomatium* spp.) was the most common native forb. Dalmatian toadflax, Russian knapweed (*Acroptilon repens*), and spotted/diffuse knapweed were sparsely scattered across the monitoring site. Toadflax was the most abundant of the noxious weeds present and the only noxious weed encountered within plots.

We identified 10 plots within the Crescent Bay monitoring site as depicting good condition (Figure 3). Most plots had big sagebrush and all had low cover of cheatgrass with a few including bulbous bluegrass. A few plots had high cover of bluebunch wheatgrass, and Sandberg's bluegrass and needlegrass were present at low cover at most plots. The good condition plots were widely scattered, an indication that good condition sagebrush steppe was not extensive within the monitoring unit.

We collected data at Crescent Bay in May 2009 from 49 plots compared to the 55 plots sampled in 2011. In 2009 we estimated cover for perennial native forbs as a group rather than separately as in 2011; so cover estimates for native forbs are not comparable between the 2 sample years (Table 3). We compared cover estimates between 2009 and 2011 for those variables that were the most abundant: exposed bare ground, big sagebrush, bluebunch wheatgrass, Sandberg's bluegrass, needlegrass, and cheatgrass. There were no significant differences of cover between years for any of these variables (all $P > 0.10$).

Table 2. <u>Crescent Bay, 2011</u>: percentage of plots (n = 55 1-m² plots) within each cover class for exposed bare ground and principal plant species organized by species guilds. Lake Roosevelt National Recreation Area.

	0	1-5%	>5-25%	>25-50%	>50-75%	>75-95%	>95-100%
Bare ground	44	51	5	0	0	0	0
Sagebrush							
Artemisia rigida	98	2	0	0	0	0	0
A.tridentata	44	22	18	10	4	2	0
A. tripartita	98	2	0	0	0	0	0
Shrubs							
Chrysothamnus viscidiflorus	98	0	2	0	0	0	0
Ericameria nauseosa	98	0	2	0	0	0	0
Leptodactylon pungens	96	2	2	0	0	0	0
Purshia tridentata	98	0	0	2	0	0	0
Salvia dorrii	98	0	0	2	0	0	0
Tetradymia glabrata	96	0	4	0	0	0	0
Native Perennial Grasses							
Poa secunda	56	42	2	0	0	0	0
Pseudoroegneria spicata	73	7	9	7	4	0	0
Sporobolus cryptandrus	98	2	0	0	0	0	0
Stipa spp.	53	22	23	2	0	0	0
Native Persistent Forbs							
Achillea millefolium	96	4	0	0	0	0	0
Artemisa dracunculus	96	4	0	0	0	0	0
Astragalus spp	96	4	0	0	0	0	0
Balsamorhiza sagittata	94	0	4	0	2	0	0
Eriogonum spp.	89	9	2	0	0	0	0
Lomatium spp.	73	21	4	2	0	0	0
Lupinus spp.	94	4	2	0	0	0	0
Phlox spp.	98	2	0	0	0	0	0
Native Other Forbs							
Alliums spp.	98	2	0	0	0	0	0
Brodiaea douglasii	96	4	0	0	0	0	0
Delphinium spp.	98	2	0	0	0	0	0
Non-native Invasive Forbs							
Erodium cicutarium	98	2	0	0	0	0	0
Linaria dalmatica	94	4	2	0	0	0	0
Non-native Invasive Grasses							
Bromus japonicus	91	7	2	0	0	0	0
B. tectorum	0	24	42	22	7	5	0
Poa bulbosa	93	5	2	0	0	0	0

Table 3. Crescent Bay, 2009: percentage of plots (n = 49 1-m² plots) within each cover class for exposed bare ground and principal plant species organized by species guilds. Lake Roosevelt National Recreation Area.

	0	1-5%	>5-25%	>25-50%	>50-75%	>75-95%	>95-100%
Bare ground	37	49	12	2	0	0	0
Sagebrush							
Artemisia tridentata	45	14	8	23	6	4	0
A. tripartita	98	0	0	0	2	0	0
Shrubs							
Chrysothamnus viscidiflorus	96	0	4	0	0	0	0
Purshia tridentata	88	2	6	2	2	0	0
Tetradymia glabrata	98	0	2	0	0	0	0
Native Perennial Grasses							
Poa secunda	59	29	6	6	0	0	0
Pseudoroegneria spicata	76	6	10	4	4	0	0
Stipa spp.	62	10	24	4	0	0	0
Forbs							
Forbs	26	31	29	8	6	0	0
Non-native Invasive Forbs							
Acroptilon repens	96	2	0	2	0	0	0
Linaria dalmatica	98	2	0	0	0	0	0
Non-native Invasive Grasses							
B. tectorum	20	16	14	32	10	8	0

Neal Canyon

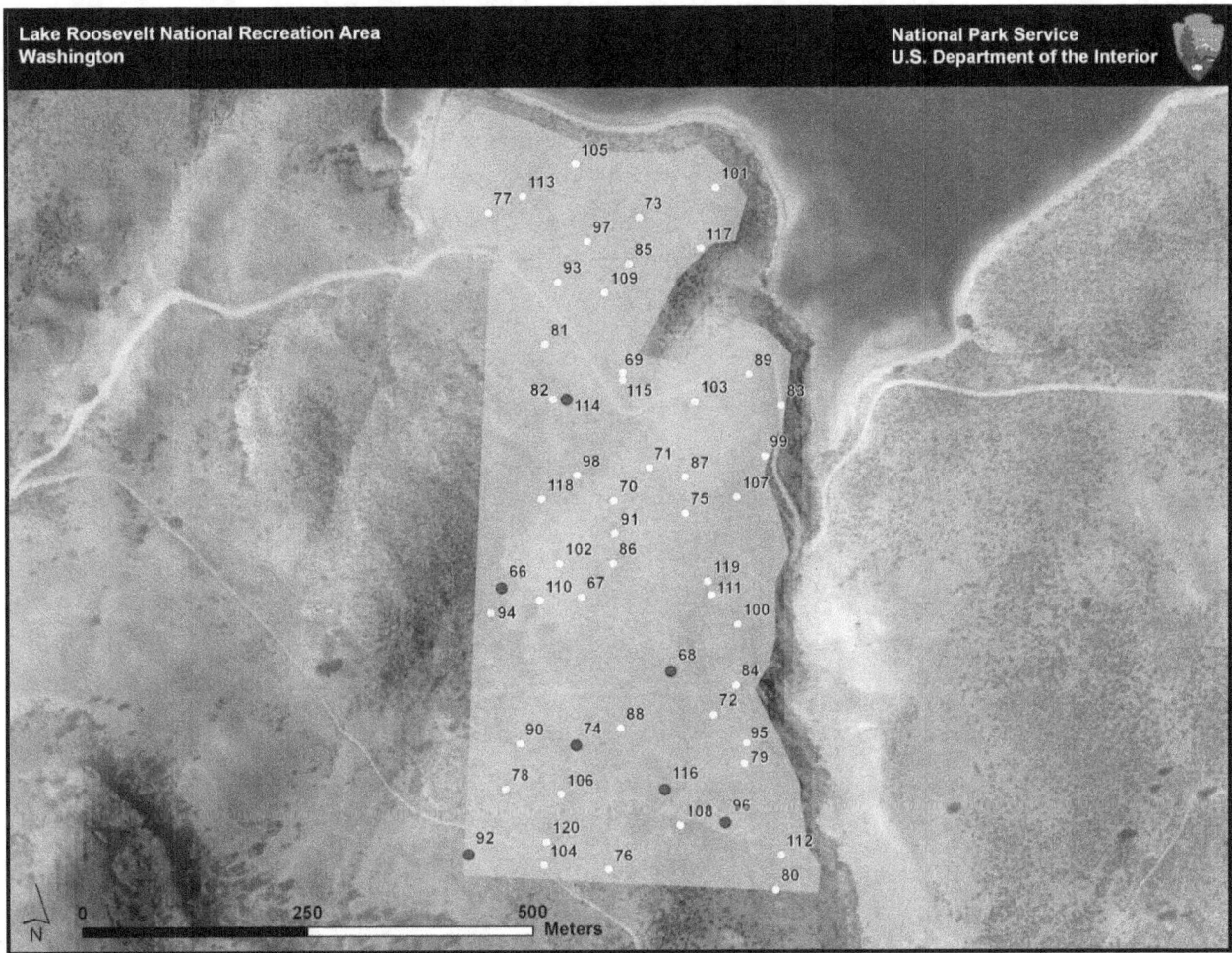

Figure 4. Neal Canyon monitoring site showing 2011 plot locations and plot numbers. Good condition plots are depicted by larger blue dots.

We sampled Neal Canyon on June 3, 2011 (Figure 4). Cheatgrass was ubiquitous across the site (99% frequency of occurrence) with generally abundant cover (56% of plots had > 25% cover, Table 4). Other annual non-native grasses, Japanese brome and bulbous bluegrass, also were present at generally low cover. Bitterbrush (*Purshia tridentata*) was the most abundant shrub with threetip sagebrush and grey rabbitbrush (*Ericamerica nauseosa*) providing additional although sparse cover across most of the site. Native bunchgrass cover also was generally low with Idaho fescue, bluebunch wheatgrass, Sandberg's bluegrass, and needlegrass as the principal species. By happenstance, we encountered the permittee on the site the day we sampled which also coincided with moving cattle from the allotment (the site had been grazed since April). The permittee's family has grazed on the area for multiple generations, and he thought that native bunchgrass cover had declined on the area over many decades. Forbs were diverse but contributed little cover; lupine (*Lupinus* spp.), yarrow (*Achillea millefolium*), and buckwheat (*Eriogonum* spp.) were the principal forbs. We did not encounter noxious weeds in any plots or observe them while walking the site.

11

Seven plots were considered in good condition (Figure 4). These were a mix of bitterbrush and threetip sagebrush with a variety of forbs and bunchgrasses. All except one had low cover of cheatgrass.

Table 4. <u>Neal Canyon, 2011</u>: percentage of plots (n = 55 1-m² plots) within each cover class for exposed bare ground and principal plant species organized by species guilds. Lake Roosevelt National Recreation Area.

	0	1-5%	>5-25%	>25-50%	>50-75%	>75-95%	>95-100%
Bare ground	69	27	4	0	0	0	0
Sagebrush							
A. tripartita	82	5	9	2	2	0	0
Shrubs							
Chrysothamnus viscidiflorus	89	0	9	2	0	0	0
Ericameria nauseosa	82	9	5	4	0	0	0
Leptodactylon pungens	98	2	0	0	0	0	0
Purshia tridentata	58	4	13	16	7	2	0
Native Perennial Grasses							
Elymus cinereus	98	0	0	2	0	0	0
Festuca idahoensis	90	5	5	0	0	0	0
Poa secunda	73	25	2	0	0	0	0
Pseudoroegneria spicata	90	5	5	0	0	0	0
Stipa spp.	82	13	5	0	0	0	0
Native Persistent Forbs							
Achillea millefolium	68	25	7	0	0	0	0
Artemisa dracunculus	78	22	0	0	0	0	0
Astragalus spp	98	2	0	0	0	0	0
Balsamorhiza sagittata	96	2	2	0	0	0	0
Cirsium spp.	98	2	0	0	0	0	0
Comandra umbellate	93	7	0	0	0	0	0
Crepis acuminate	98	2	0	0	0	0	0
Erigeron spp.	96	2	2	0	0	0	0
Eriogonum spp.	72	15	9	2	2	0	0
Lithospermum ruderale	98	2	0	0	0	0	0
Lomatium spp.	91	9	0	0	0	0	0
Lupinus spp.	54	35	9	2	0	0	0
Opuntia polyacantha	96	2	2	0	0	0	0
Phlox spp.	93	7	0	0	0	0	0
Non-native Invasive Forbs							
Descurainia spp.	98	2	0	0	0	0	0
Sisymbrium altissimum	98	2	0	0	0	0	0
Non-native Invasive Grasses							
Bromus japonicus	94	4	2	0	0	0	0
B. tectorum	2	11	31	37	15	4	0
Poa bulbosa	83	15	2	0	0	0	0
Poa pratensis	98	2	0	0	0	0	0

Ponderosa

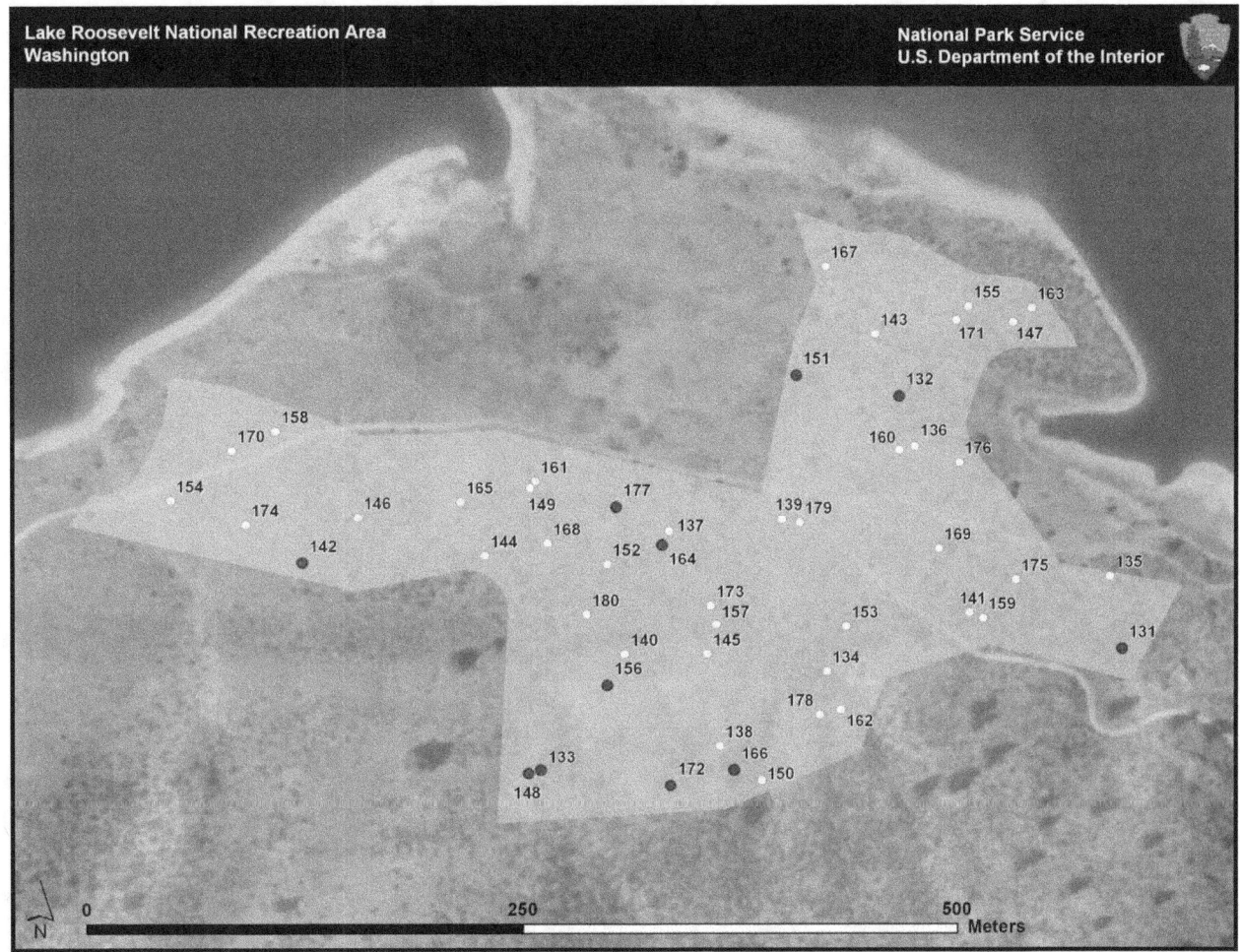

Figure 5. Ponderosa monitoring site showing 2011 plot locations and plot numbers. Good condition plots are depicted by larger blue dots.

We sampled the Ponderosa sample frame on June 2, 2011 (Figure 5). This site is part of a grazing allotment although we did not notice evidence of recent livestock grazing.

As found on the other monitoring sites, cheatgrass was the most common plant encountered (94% frequency) with 38% of plots having > 25% cover (Table 5). Japanese brome and bulbous bluegrass occasionally contributed more than 5% to the cover of a plot. Shrub cover was principally comprised of bitterbrush and threetip sagebrush. Big sagebrush was much less abundant. Other shrubs included grey and green rabbitbrushes (*Chrysothamnus viscidiflorus*), serviceberry (*Amelanchier alnifolia*), gooseberry (*Ribes* spp.), and rose (*Rosa* spp.; although rose was not encountered in plots). Needlegrass and Sandberg's bluegrass were the principal native perennial grasses although generally cover was low. There was a small stand of Idaho fescue on a northerly aspect, and bluebunch wheatgrass in good condition south of the main road that passes through the monitoring site (Figure 6). Yarrow and lupine were the principal native forbs with a few other forbs occurring occasionally. There were few non-native invasive forbs. Exposed soil cover was low as a result of the high cover of annual grasses and litter. There was knapweed (either *Centaurea diffusa* or *C. maculosa*) on the main road through the site but no noxious weeds were encountered within plots.

We identified 11 plots as good condition (Figure 5). These plots were a mix of threetip sagebrush and bitterbrush with understories of diverse grasses and forbs. Several of these plots plots had high cover (≥ 50%) of Idaho fescue or bluebunch wheatgrass. Annual grasses were present on all but 3 of the good condition plots.

Figure 6. Healthy stand of vigorous Idaho fescue and bluebunch wheatgrass on the Ponderosa monitoring site, looking southeast from plot #140.
Although mostly dominated by native plants, cheatgrass still was common within this stand.

Table 5. Ponderosa, 2011: percentage of plots (n = 50 1-m² plots) within each cover class for exposed bare ground and principal plant species organized by species guilds. Lake Roosevelt National Recreation Area.

	0	1-5%	>5-25%	>25-50%	>50-75%	>75-95%	95-100%
Bare ground	72	28	0	0	0	0	0
Sagebrush							
Artemisia tridentata	92	0	2	4	2	0	0
A. tripartita	58	16	20	6	0	0	0
Shrubs							
Amelanchier alnifolia	96	0	2	2	0	0	0
Chrysothamnus viscidiflorus	92	6	2	0	0	0	0
Ericameria nauseosa	78	6	10	4	2	0	0
Purshia tridentata	58	6	8	14	6	10	0
Ribes spp.	98	0	0	0	2	0	0
Native Perennial Grasses							
Elymus cinereus	98	2	0	0	0	0	0
Festuca idahoensis	90	0	6	2	2	0	0
Poa secunda	74	26	0	0	0	0	0
Pseudoroegneria spicata	94	4	0	2	0	0	0
Stipa spp.	60	30	10	0	0	0	0
Native Persistent Forbs							
Achillea millefolium	56	38	6	0	0	0	0
Artemisa dracunculus	72	28	0	0	0	0	0
Comandra umbellata	92	8	0	0	0	0	0
Eriogonum spp.	84	16	0	0	0	0	0
Lithospermum ruderale	84	14	2	0	0	0	0
Lomatium spp.	92	8	0	0	0	0	0
Lupinus spp.	64	30	6	0	0	0	0
Phlox spp.	98	2	0	0	0	0	0
Senecio spp.	94	6	0	0	0	0	0
Native Other Forbs							
Brodiaea douglasii	98	2	0	0	0	0	0
Delphinium spp.	98	2	0	0	0	0	0
Non-native Invasive Forbs							
Descurainia spp.	92	8	0	0	0	0	0
Erodium cicutarium	98	2	0	0	0	0	0
Sisymbrium altissimum	98	2	0	0	0	0	0
Non-native Invasive Grasses							
Bromus japonicus	68	22	10	0	0	0	0
B. tectorum	6	24	32	30	6	2	0
Poa bulbosa	68	26	6	0	0	0	0

Spring Canyon East

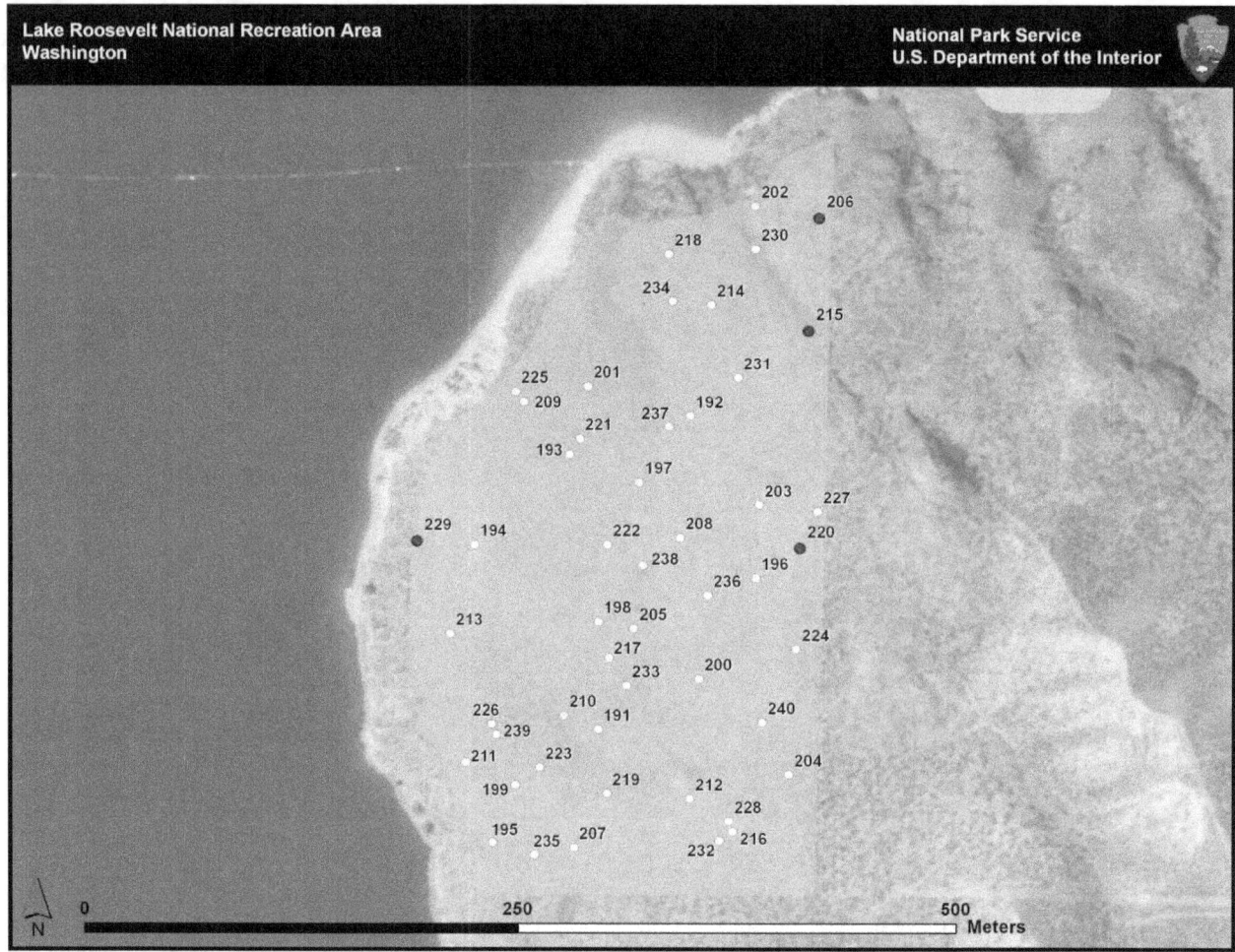

Figure 7. Spring Canyon East monitoring site showing 2011 plot locations and plot numbers. Good condition plots are depicted by larger blue dots.

We sampled Spring Canyon East on June 5, 2011 (Figure 7). This monitoring site is grazed by cattle although recent livestock grazing was not evident at the time of sampling. Cheatgrass was common, with 60% of the plots having > 25% cover (Table 6). Japanese brome also contributed substantial cover in some plots. Big sagebrush and bitterbrush were the principal shrubs. Sandberg's bluegrass was the principal native bunchgrass. Native forb cover was low; buckwheat and bisquitroot were the most abundant native forbs. No noxious weeds were encountered in plots but Dalmatian toadflax and knapweed (either spotted or diffuse) were sparsely scattered with most observed close to the southern boundary of the site.

Four plots were identified as in good condition (Figure 7). All 4 plots had low cover of annual grasses, and none had high cover of native bunchgrasses. But there was a mix of native grasses, forbs, and shrubs at low cover on these 4 plots.

16

We sampled Spring Canyon East in May 2009 (n = 51 plots; Table 7). Plant cover of the most abundant species – big sagebrush, bitterbrush, Sandberg's bluegrass, and cheatgrass – were similar between years. Exposed soil cover was greater in 2009 than 2011 ($P < 0.001$).

Table 6. <u>Spring Canyon East, 2011</u>: percentage of plots (n = 50 1-m² plots) within each cover class for exposed bare ground and principal plant species organized by species guilds. Lake Roosevelt National Recreation Area.

	0	1-5%	>5-25%	>25-50%	>50-75%	>75-95%	>95-100%
Bare ground	66	30	4	0	0	0	0
Sagebrush							
Artemisia tridentata	50	20	14	12	4	0	0
Shrubs							
Chrysothamnus viscidiflorus	94	2	4	0	0	0	0
Ericameria nauseosa	94	4	2	0	0	0	0
Purshia tridentata	62	14	16	6	0	2	0
Salvia dorrii	98	0	0	0	2	0	0
Native Perennial Grasses							
Festuca idahoensis	98	2	0	0	0	0	0
Poa secunda	50	42	8	0	0	0	0
Pseudoroegneria spicata	92	4	2	2	0	0	0
Stipa spp.	92	6	2	0	0	0	0
Native Persistent Forbs							
Achillea millefolium	96	4	0	0	0	0	0
Balsamorhiza sagittata	98	2	0	0	0	0	0
Eriogonum spp.	86	12	2	0	0	0	0
Lomatium spp.	90	10	0	0	0	0	0
Lupinus spp.	96	4	0	0	0	0	0
Phlox spp.	98	2	0	0	0	0	0
Native Other Forbs							
Brodiaea douglasii	98	2	0	0	0	0	0
Calochortus spp.	98	2	0	0	0	0	0
Delphinium spp.	98	2	0	0	0	0	0
Zigadenus spp.	98	2	0	0	0	0	0
Non-native Invasive Forbs							
Descurainia spp.	94	6	0	0	0	0	0
Erodium cicutarium	98	2	0	0	0	0	0
Non-native Invasive Grasses							
Bromus japonicus	68	14	12	6	0	0	0
B. tectorum	4	16	20	24	28	8	0
Poa bulbosa	86	12	2	0	0	0	0

Table 7. <u>Spring Canyon East, 2009</u>: percentage of plots (n = 51 1-m² plots) within each cover class for exposed bare ground and principal plant species organized by species guilds. Lake Roosevelt National Recreation Area.

	0	1-5%	>5-25%	>25-50%	>50-75%	>75-95%	>95-100%
Bare ground	16	41	25	14	2	2	0
Sagebrush							
Artemisia rigida	98	2	0	0	0	0	0
A. tridentata	63	4	16	12	2	2	2
Shrubs							
Chrysothamnus viscidiflorus	94	0	2	4	0	0	0
Ericameria nauseosa	94	4	0	2	0	0	0
Purshia tridentata	58	6	12	16	6	0	2
Salvia dorrii	94	4	2	0	0	0	0
Native Perennial Grasses							
Festuca idahoensis	98	2	0	0	0	0	0
Poa secunda	41	37	18	4	0	0	0
Pseudoroegneria spicata	92	6	2	0	0	0	0
Stipa spp.	90	10	0	0	0	0	0
Forbs							
Forbs	42	44	14	0	0	0	0
Non-native Invasive Grasses							
B. tectorum	2	24	30	20	16	8	0

Spring Canyon West

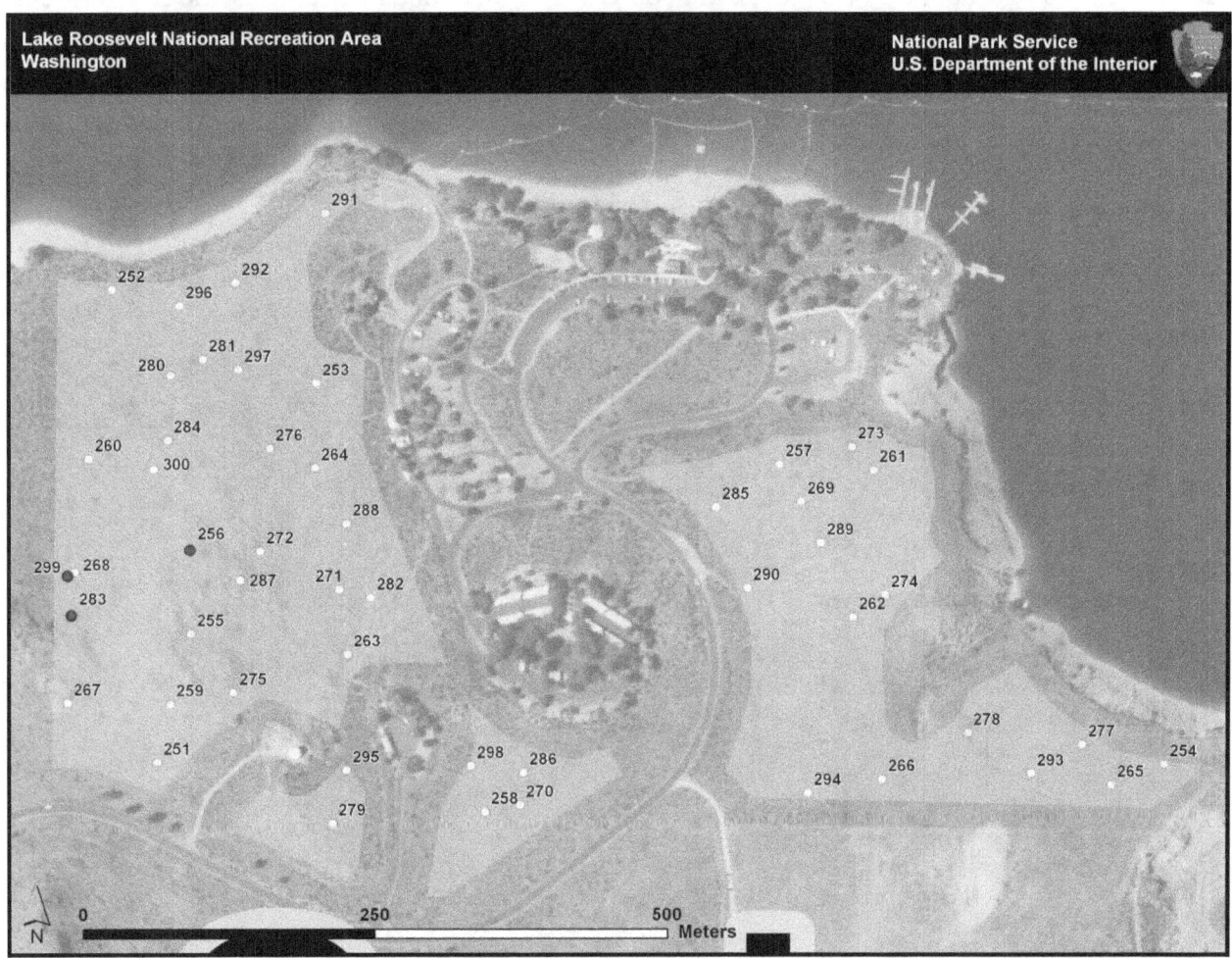

Figure 8. Spring Canyon West monitoring site showing 2011 plot locations and plot numbers. Good condition plots are depicted by larger blue dots.

We sampled Spring Canyon West on June 1, 2011 (Figure 8). This area borders the Spring Canyon campground on 3 sides and includes a nature trail through portions of the monitoring site. Cheatgrass, as was the case in all sample frames, was the most commonly encountered species with the most cover (96% frequency; Table 8). Green rabbitbrush, grey rabbitbrush, and bitterbrush were the principal shrubs. Sagebrush cover was sparse. Sandberg's bluegrass and needlegrass were the principal bunchgrasses although bluebunch wheatgrass had good cover in a few plots. Native forbs generally were common although cover was low. Buckwheat and wormwood (*Artemisia dracunculus*) were the most commonly encountered forbs. Dalmatian toadflax was visually common and widely dispersed throughout the site although cover generally was low (only 1 plot with cover > 5%). I encountered a single Russian knapweed plant in 1 plot. Crested wheatgrass was more common here than at other monitoring sites, mostly on the east side of the site.

We identified 3 plots in good condition (Figure 8). Threetip sagebrush and green rabbitbrush dominated the 3 locations. Two plots had good cover of bluebunch wheatgrass and Idaho fescue. Cheatgrass had low cover on 2 of the plots.

We sampled Spring Canyon West in May 2009. Cover estimates for exposed soil, green rabbitbrush, grey rabbitbrush, and needlegrass were higher in 2009 than in 2011 (P ≤ 0.10; Tables 8 & 9). Bitterbrush and Sandberg's bluegrass cover was similar in 2009 and 2011. Cheatgrass cover was greater in 2011 than in 2009.

Table 8. Spring Canyon West, 2011: percentage of plots (n = 50 1-m² plots) within each cover class for exposed bare ground and principal plant species organized by species guilds. Lake Roosevelt National Recreation Area.

	0	1-5%	>5-25%	>25-50%	>50-75%	>75-95%	>95-100%
Bare ground	54	46	0	0	0	0	0
Sagebrush							
Artemisia tridentata	98	0	0	2	0	0	0
A. tripartita	96	0	2	0	0	2	0
Shrubs							
Chrysothamnus viscidiflorus	64	10	20	6	0	0	0
Ericameria nauseosa	70	14	14	2	0	0	0
Gutierrezia sarothrae	94	6	0	0	0	0	0
Purshia tridentata	78	6	10	4	2	0	0
Native Perennial Grasses							
Festuca idahoensis	98	0	2	0	0	0	0
Oryzopsis hymenoides	98	2	0	0	0	0	0
Poa secunda	60	34	6	0	0	0	0
Pseudoroegneria spicata	86	2	4	8	0	0	0
Sporobolus cryptandrus	98	0	2	0	0	0	0
Stipa spp.	62	10	18	10	0	0	0
Native Persistent Forbs							
Achillea millefolium	80	18	2	0	0	0	0
Artemisia dracunculus	78	18	4	0	0	0	0
Balsamorhiza sagittata	86	10	4	0	0	0	0
Comandra umbellate	86	14	0	0	0	0	0
Crepis acuminata	94	6	0	0	0	0	0
Eriogonum spp.	76	22	2	0	0	0	0
Eriophyllum lanatum	98	2	0	0	0	0	0
Hymenopappus filifolius	98	2	0	0	0	0	0
Lithospermum ruderale	98	0	2	0	0	0	0
Lomatium spp.	96	4	0	0	0	0	0
Lupinus spp.	94	6	0	0	0	0	0
Opuntia polyacantha	96	4	0	0	0	0	0
Phlox spp.	84	16	0	0	0	0	0
Non-native Invasive Forbs							
Acroptilon repens	98	2	0	0	0	0	0
Erodium cicutarium	96	4	0	0	0	0	0
Linaria dalmatica	90	8	2	0	0	0	0
Sisymbrium altissimum	98	2	0	0	0	0	0
Non-native Invasive Grasses							
Agropyron cristatum	82	6	6	6	0	0	0
B. tectorum	4	6	34	32	12	12	0
Poa bulbosa	88	6	6	0	0	0	0

Table 9. <u>Spring Canyon West, 2009</u>: percentage of plots (n = 50 1-m² plots) within each cover class for exposed bare ground and principal plant species by species guilds. Lake Roosevelt National Recreation Area.

	0	1-5%	>5-25%	>25-50%	>50-75%	>75-95%	>95-100%
Bare ground	14	60	26	0	0	0	0
Sagebrush							
A. tripartita	94	0	4	2	0	0	0
Shrubs							
Chrysothamnus viscidiflorus	58	18	18	4	2	0	0
Ericameria nauseosa	76	12	8	4	0	0	0
Juniperus communis	98	2	0	0	0	0	0
Purshia tridentate	74	8	6	8	2	2	0
Rosa spp.	98	0	2	0	0	0	0
Native Perennial Grasses							
Festuca idahoensis	96	0	4	0	0	0	0
Oryzopsis hymenoides	96	0	4	0	0	0	0
Poa secunda	36	48	16	0	0	0	0
Pseudoroegneria spicata	90	0	6	2	2	0	0
Sporobolus cryptandrus	98	0	2	0	0	0	0
Stipa spp.	66	12	16	6	0	0	0
Forbs							
Forbs	20	52	26	2	0	0	0
Non-native Invasive Forbs							
Linaria dalmatica	90	10	0	0	0	0	0
Non-native Invasive Grasses							
Agropyron cristatum	88	4	4	2	0	2	0
B. tectorum	0	28	24	34	8	6	0

As is common across sagebrush steppe in the Upper Columbia Basin, cheatgrass dominated these communities at LARO. Frequencies of occurrence ranged from 94 – 100% at the 5 sites. Median cheatgrass cover at Spring Canyon East, Spring Canyon West, and Neal Canyon was higher than at Ponderosa or Crescent Bay ($P < 0.006$). Due to the wet, mild spring of 2011, annual grasses likely produced high cover values. Other non-native annual grasses, i.e., Japanese brome and bulbous bluegrass, although much less abundant than cheatgrass, were regularly encountered as well.

Abundance of noxious weeds varied among the 5 monitoring sites. Despite being visually obvious, particularly at Spring Canyon West, estimated cover of noxious weeds typically was low at all sites. Still, noxious weeds are widely present in sagebrush steppe in the park and pose an ongoing challenge for LARO management.

Thirty-five plots of the 260 sampled (13%) were deemed in good condition. Good condition was defined as an absence of noxious weeds, low cover of invasive annual grasses, and lower cover of exposed soil. This is not to say these plots supported vigorous and diverse understories of native forbs and grasses. Rather that these plots at least supported predominately native species, and roughly depict the character of true sagebrush steppe. This presents the hope for the plant community resistance to non-native plant invasion, and the possibility of restoring larger swaths of sagebrush steppe to healthier communities.

Two sites, Crescent Bay and Spring Canyon West, may provide opportunities for the park to maintain and restore stands of mostly native vegetation that could represent to the public what these hillsides once supported. A nature trail already exists at Spring Canyon West, and possibly a similar trail might be constructed at Crescent Bay (J. Weaver, NPS, 2009, pers. comm.). But the large presence of recreational use at Spring Canyon West, coupled with the existing widespread presence of Dalmatian toadflax, will make maintaining and expanding native sagebrush steppe there particularly challenging.

The other 3 monitoring sites are more isolated from park visitors and are part of cattle grazing allotments. As noted for the Ponderosa site, there still remain isolated pockets of healthy, mostly native sagebrush steppe vegetation. Careful grazing management and this monitoring program can complement each other in maintaining and possibly expanding these healthy stands.

Boundaries of 3 monitoring sites – Crescent Bay, Neal Canyon, and Spring Canyon West – will be modified slightly for future sampling to exclude some rock outcrops and steep, treacherous terrain, although this will not impact the placement of plots in the future for comparison with past monitoring.

Literature Cited

Daubenmire, R. F. 1959. A canopy-coverage method. Northwest Science **33**:43-64.

Garrett, L. K., T. J. Rodhouse, G. H. Dicus, C. C. Caudill, and M. R. Shardlow. 2007. Upper Columbia Basin Network vital signs monitoring plan. Natural Resource Report NPS/UCBN/NRR-2007/002. National Park Service, Fort Collins, Colorado.

Higgins, J. J. 2004. An introduction to modern nonparametric statistics. Brooks/Cole – Thomson Learning, Pacific Grove, California.

Rodhouse, T. J. 2010. Sagebrush steppe vegetation monitoring in Craters of the Moon National Monument and Preserve, Hagerman Fossil Beds National Monument, John Day Fossil Beds National Monument, and Lake Roosevelt National Recreation Area: 2009 annual report. Natural Resource Technical Report NPS/UCBN/NRTR—2010/302. National Park Service, Fort Collins, Colorado.

Stevens, D. L., and A. R. Olsen. 2004. Spatially balanced sampling of natural resources. Journal of the American Statistical Association **99**:262-278.

Walter, H., E. Harnickell, and D. Mueller-Dombois. 1975. Climate-diagram maps of the individual continents and the ecological climatic regions of the earth. Springer-Verlag, Berlin.

Western Regional Climate Center. 2011. Western U.S. Climate Historical Summaries. Accessed at: http://www.wrcc.dri.edu/Climsum.html.

Yeo, J. J., T. J. Rodhouse, G. H. Dicus, K. M. Irvine, and L. K. Garrett. 2009. Upper Columbia Basin Network sagebrush steppe vegetation monitoring protocol: Narrative version 1.0. Natural Resource Report NPS/UCBN/NRR—2009/142. National Park Service, Fort Collins, Colorado.

Appendix A. List of plant species mentioned in the report with common and scientific names

Common Name	Species Name
Sagebrush	
Rigid sagebrush	*Artemisia rigida*
Big sagebrush	*Artemisia tridentata*
Threetip sagebrush	*Artemisia tripartita*
Shrubs	
Serviceberry	*Amelanchier alnifolia*
Green rabbitbrush	*Chrysothamnus viscidiflorus*
Grey rabbitbrush	*Ericamerica nauseosa*
Broom snakeweed	*Gutierrezia sarothrae*
Common juniper	*Juniperus communis*
Prickly phlox	*Leptodactylon pungens*
Bitterbrush	*Purshia tridentata*
Rose	*Rosa spp.*
Purple sage	*Salvia dorrii*
Horsebrush	*Tetradymia glabrata*
Native Perennial Grasses	
Basin wildrye	*Elymus cinereus*
Idaho fescue	*Festuca idahoensis*
Indian ricegrass	*Oryzopsis hymenoides*
Sandberg's bluegrass	*Poa secunda*
Bluebunch wheatgrass	*Pseudoroegneria spicata*
Sand dropseed	*Sporobolus cryptandrus*
Needlegrass	*Stipa spp.*
Native Persistent Forbs	
Yarrow	*Achillea millefolium*
Tarragon	*Artemisia dracunculus*
Milk-vetch	*Astragalus spp.*
Arrowleaf balsamroot	*Balsamorhiza sagittata*
Native thistle	*Cirsium spp.*
Bastard toadflax	*Comandra umbellata*
Tapertip hawksbeard	*Crepis accuminata*
Daisy	*Erigeron spp.*
Buckwheat	*Eriogonum spp.*
Woolly sunflower	*Eriophyllum lanatum*
Fineleaf hymenopappus	*Hymenopappus filifolius*
Western stoneseed	*Lithospermum ruderale*
Desert parsley	*Lomatium spp.*
Lupine	*Lupinus spp.*
Prickly pear cactus	*Opuntia polyacantha*
Phlox	*Phlox spp.*
Groundsel	*Senecio spp.*
Native Other Forbs	
Onion	*Allium spp.*
Douglas' brodiaea	*Brodiaea douglasii*
Larkspur	*Delphinium spp.*
Death camas	*Zigadenus spp.*
Non-native Invasive Forbs	
Russian knapweed	*Acroptilon repens*

Appendix A. List of plant species mentioned in the report with common and scientific names (continued).

Common Name	Species Name
Tansy mustard	*Descurainia spp.*
Filaree	*Erodium cicutarium*
Dalmatian toadflax	*Linaria dalmatica*
Tumble mustard	*Sisymbrium altissimum*
Non-native Invasive Grasses	
Crested wheatgrass	*Agropyron cristatum*
Japanese brome	*Bromus japonicus*
Cheatgrass	*Bromus tectorum*
Bulbous bluegrass	*Poa bulbosa*
Kentucky bluegrass	*Poa pratensis*